VOGUE® KNITTING

PONCHOS

VOGUE KNITTING
PONCHOS

SIXTH&SPRING BOOKS
NEW YORK

SIXTH&SPRING BOOKS
233 Spring Street
New York, New York 10013

Library of Congress Cataloging-in-Publication Data

Library of Congress Control Number: 2005920084

ISBN: 1-931543-79-8
ISBN-13: 978-1-931543-79-8

Manufactured in China

1 3 5 7 9 10 8 6 4 2

First Edition

TABLE OF CONTENTS

INTRODUCTION

After years of coming in second to the illustrious sweater, the poncho is finally getting its due. Perfect for multiseason wear, lacking pesky sleeves and shaping, and flattering on a range of body types, it has liberated a whole new generation of knitters and knitwear enthusiasts with its versatility and accessibility. Who needs a sweater when you can have a poncho?

Well, that may be going a bit far, but certainly the poncho is giving people a whole new outlook on covering up. Whether you're using cotton or wool, strolling the boardwalk or hustling across town, the poncho is a great alternative to the more traditional garments we have come to know and love. And with such a freeform structure, it is a friendly next step for those novices who are ready for a new challenge but are not yet committed to the demands of a sweater or jacket.

Of course, that's not to say that all kinds of knitters can't enjoy the trend. We've thought of a whole range of levels and tastes in compiling this collection, and we're excited that so many will be able to embark on the projects in our pages, from the elegant mohair and mesh designs to the more rustic cabled and fisherman's fare. There are even a few kid's styles to ensure that no one is left out.

So put down your sweater pattern, flip through our pages, and get ready to **KNIT ON THE GO!**

THE BASICS

Who can resist the easy, breezy style of a knit poncho? Aside from their inherent good looks, ponchos are approachable projects for all knitters because of the variety of ways in which they're made and finished: Some are stockinette stitch, others are cabled; some are seamed, others are knit in the round; some hang straight, others on the bias. In short, ponchos are for everyone, no matter the taste or ability—just take a look!

SIZING

Many of the ponchos in this book are written in one size. The key elements of fit are the neck opening, width around at the shoulder, and the total length. The shoulder measurement of an adult does not vary as greatly as the bust measurement; therefore, it is not as necessary to have a large size range. Changing the length is quite easy, especially since most of the ponchos are knit from the neck down. Therefore, you can try on the poncho as you are knitting and adjust the length if necessary.

CONSTRUCTION

One of the most common methods of knitting a poncho is in one piece from the neck down, such as the Ribbon Capelet on page 60. You can also knit in one piece from the lower edge up to the neck, as in the Ribbed Poncho on page 38. It is best to use a circular needle for both of these versions, to easily accommodate the large number of stitches. Another method is to knit from the neck down, but in two pieces—front and back, as in the Aran Poncho on page 68—in which case you will have to sew the side and shoulder seams. Another popular style, especially for beginning knitters, is a simple rectangle (or two rectangles) seamed together to form the poncho, as in the Bobble Poncho on page 29.

YARN SELECTION

For an exact reproduction of the projects shown in this book, use the yarn listed in the Materials section of the pattern. We've chosen yarns that are readily available in the U.S. and Canada at the time of printing. The Resources list on pages 86 and 87 provides addresses of yarn distributors. Contact them for the name of a retailer in your area.

YARN SUBSTITUTION

You may wish to substitute yarns. Perhaps you view small-scale projects as a chance to incorporate leftovers from your yarn stash,

It is always important to knit a gauge swatch, and it is even more so with garments to ensure proper fit.

Patterns usually state gauge over a 4"/10cm span; however, it's beneficial to make a larger test swatch. This gives you a more precise stitch gauge, a better idea of the appearance and drape of the knitted fabric, and a chance to familiarize yourself with the stitch pattern.

The type of needles used—straight or circular, wood or metal—will influence gauge, so knit your swatch with the needles you plan to use for the project. Measure gauge as illustrated. Try different needle sizes until your sample measures the required number of stitches and rows. *To get fewer stitches to the inch/cm, use larger needles; to get more stitches to the inch/cm, use smaller needles.*

Knitting in the round may tighten the gauge, so if you measured the gauge on a flat swatch, take another gauge reading after you begin knitting. When the piece measures at least 2"/5cm, lay it flat and measure over the stitches in the center of the piece, as the side stitches may be distorted.

It's a good idea to keep your gauge swatch in order to test blocking and cleaning methods.

or maybe the yarn specified is not available in your area. You'll need to knit to the given gauge to obtain the knitted measurements with a substitute yarn (see "Gauge," above). Be sure to consider how the fiber content of the substitute yarn will affect the comfort and the ease of care of your projects.

To facilitate yarn substitution, *Vogue Knitting* grades yarn by the standard stitch gauge obtained in stockinette stitch. You'll find a grading number in the Materials section of the pattern, immediately following the fiber type of the yarn. Look for a substitute yarn that falls into the same category. The suggested needle size and gauge on the yarn label should be comparable to that on the Standard Yarn Weight chart (see page 12).

After you've successfully gauge-swatched a substitute yarn, you'll need to

Categories of yarn, gauge ranges, and recommended needle and hook sizes

Yarn Weight Symbol & Category Names	1 Super Fine	2 Fine	3 Light	4 Medium	5 Bulky	6 Super Bulky
Type of Yarns in Category	Sock, Fingering, Baby	Sport, Baby	DK, Light Worsted	Worsted, Afghan, Aran	Chunky, Craft, Rug	Bulky, Roving
Knit Gauge Range* in Stockinette Stitch to 4 Inches	27–32 sts	23–26 sts	21–24 sts	16–20 sts	12–15 sts	6–11 sts
Recommended Needle in Metric Size Range	2.25–3.25 mm	3.25–3.75 mm	3.75–4.5 mm	4.5–5.5 mm	5.5–8 mm	8 mm and larger
Recommended Needle U.S. Size Range	1 to 3	3 to 5	5 to 7	7 to 9	9 to 11	11 and larger
Crochet Gauge* Ranges in Single Crochet To 4 Inch	21–32 sts	16–20 sts	12–17 sts	11–14 sts	8–11 sts	5–9 sts
Recommended Hook in Metric Size Range	2.25–3.5 mm	3.5–4.5 mm	4.5–5.5 mm	5.5–6.5 mm	6.5–9 mm	9 mm and larger
Recommended Hook U.S. Size Range	B–1 to E–4	E–4 to 7	7 to I–9	I–9 to K–10½	K–10½ to M–13	M–13 and larger

*Guidelines only: The above reflects the most commonly used needle or hook sizes for specific yarn categories.

SKILL LEVELS FOR KNITTING

■□□□

Beginner
Ideal first project.

■■□□

Very Easy Very Vogue
Basic stitches, minimal shaping, simple finishing.

■■■□

Intermediate
For knitters with some experience. More intricate stitches, shaping, and finishing.

■■■■

Experienced
For knitters able to work patterns with complicated shaping and finishing.

figure out how much of the substitute yarn the project requires. First, find the total length of the original yarn in the pattern (multiply number of balls by yards/meters per ball). Divide this figure by the new yards/meters per ball (listed on the yarn label). Round up to the next whole number. The answer is the number of balls required.

FOLLOWING CHARTS

Charts are a convenient way to follow colorwork, lace, cable, and other stitch patterns at a glance. *Vogue Knitting* stitch charts utilize the universal knitting language of "symbolcraft." When knitting back and forth in rows, read charts from right to left on right side (RS) rows and from left to right on wrong side (WS) rows, repeating any stitch and row repeats as directed in the pattern. When knitting in the round, read charts from right to left on every round. Posting a self-adhesive note under your working row is an easy way to keep track of your place on a chart.

COLORWORK KNITTING

The Icelandic Poncho on page 72 uses the stranding method of colorwork: When motifs are closely placed, colorwork is accomplished by stranding along two or more colors per row, creating "floats" on the wrong side of the fabric. This technique is sometimes called Fair Isle knitting, after the traditional Fair Isle patterns that are composed of small motifs with frequent color changes.

To keep an even tension and prevent holes while knitting, pick up yarns alternately over and under one another across or around. While knitting, stretch the stitches on the needle slightly wider than the length of the float at the back, to keep work from puckering.

When changing colors at the beginning of rows or rounds, carry yarn along for a few rows only, or cut yarn and rejoin when needed. It is important to keep the floats small and neat so they don't catch when you pull the piece over your head.

BLOCKING

Blocking is an all-important finishing step in the knitting process. It is the best way to shape pattern pieces and smooth knitted edges in preparation for seaming or for a neat and even edge. If you have no seams and the fabric is already smooth and even, blocking may not be necessary. However, if you do want to block an item that was knit in the round, lay it flat and block the double thickness, being careful not to make creases if using an iron. Most items retain their shape if the blocking stages in the instructions are followed carefully. Choose a blocking method according to the yarn-care label and when in doubt, test-block your gauge swatch.

Wet Block Method

Using rust-proof pins, pin pieces to measurements on a flat surface and lightly dampen using a spray bottle. Allow to dry before removing pins.

Steam Block Method

With WS facing, pin pieces. Steam lightly, holding the iron 2"/5cm above the knitting. Do not press or it will flatten stitches.

FINISHING

After blocking, there is very little, if any, finishing on a poncho. Many times fringe is added onto the ends. You can make the fringe as short or long as you like, depending on preference or amount of leftover yarn. A crocheted edge can also be added to keep the edges from curling.

SEWING

When using a very bulky or highly textured yarn, it is sometimes easier to seam pieces together with a finer, flat yarn. Just be sure that your sewing yarn closely matches the color of the original yarn used in your project.

CARE

Refer to the yarn label for the recommended cleaning method. Many of the projects in the book can be either washed by hand or in the machine on a gentle or wool cycle, in lukewarm water with a mild detergent. Do not agitate or soak for more than ten minutes. Rinse gently with tepid water, then fold in a towel and gently squeeze out the water. Lay flat to dry away from excess heat and light. Check the yarn label for any specific care instructions, such as dry cleaning or tumble drying.

TO BEGIN SEAMING

If you have left a long tail from your cast-on row, you can use this strand to begin sewing. To make a neat join at the lower edge with no gap, use the technique shown here. Thread the strand into a yarn needle. With the right sides of both pieces facing you, insert the yarn needle from back to front into the corner stitch of the piece without the tail. Making a figure eight with the yarn, insert the needle from back to front into the stitch with the cast-on tail. Tighten to close the gap.

INVISIBLE SEAMING: STOCKINETTE ST

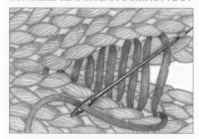

To make an invisible side seam in a garment worked in stockinette stitch, insert the yarn needle under the horizontal bar between the first and second stitches. Insert the needle into the corresponding bar on the other piece. Pull the yarn gently until the sides meet. Continue alternating from side to side.

CIRCULAR NEEDLES

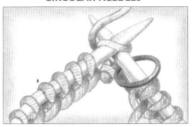

1 Hold the needle tip with the last cast-on stitch in your right hand and the tip with the first cast-on stitch in your left hand. Knit the first cast-on stitch, pulling the yarn tight to avoid a gap.

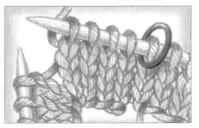

2 Work until you reach the marker. This completes the first round. Slip the marker to the right needle and work the next round.

TASSELS

Cut a piece of cardboard to the desired length of the tassel. Wrap yarn around the cardboard. Knot a piece of yarn tightly around one end, cut as shown, and remove the cardboard. Wrap and tie yarn around the tassel about 1"/2.5cm down from the top to secure the fringe.

DOUBLE-POINTED NEEDLES

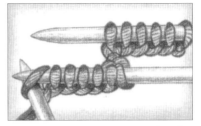

1 Cast on the required number of stitches on the first needle, plus one extra. Slip this extra stitch to the next needle as shown. Continue in this way, casting on the required number of stitches on the last needle.

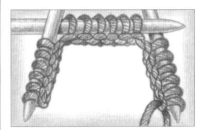

2 Arrange the needles as shown, with the cast-on edge facing the center of the triangle (or square).

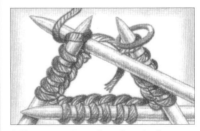

3 Place a stitch marker after the last cast-on stitch. With the free needle, knit the first cast-on stitch, pulling the yarn tightly. Continue knitting in rounds, slipping the marker before beginning each round.

The provisional cast-on, sometimes called open cast-on, is used when you want to have open stitches at the cast-on edge in order to pick up stitches later to work a hem, or if you want to weave these open stitches to the final row of stitches for a smooth seam, as in the Textured Poncho on page 79. There are many different ways to work a provisional cast-on, two of which are described below. The Textured Poncho was worked with the crochet hook method.

With a crochet hook

1 Using waste yarn of a similar weight to the project yarn and a crochet hook appropriate for that yarn, chain the number of cast-on stitches stated in the instructions. Cut a tail and pull the tail through the last chain.

2 Using the needles and working yarn, pick up one stitch through the "purl bumps" on the back of each crochet chain. Be careful not to split the waste yarn, as this makes it difficult to pull out the crochet chain at the end.

3 Continue working pattern as described.

4 To remove waste chain, pull out the tail from the last crochet stitch. Gently and slowly pull on the tail to unravel the crochet stitches, carefully placing each released knit stitch on a needle.

Long Tail

1 Leaving tails about 4"/10cm long, tie a length of scrap yarn (approximately four times the desired width) together with the main yarn in a knot. With your right hand, hold the knot on top of the needle a short distance from the tip, then place your thumb and index finger between the two yarns and hold the long ends with the other fingers. Hold your hand with your palm facing upward and spread your thumb and index finger apart so that the yarn forms a "V" with the main yarn over your index finger and the scrap yarn over your thumb.

2 Bring the needle up through the scrap-yarn loop on your thumb from front to back. Place the needle over the main yarn on your index finger and then back through the loop

on your thumb. Drop the loop off your thumb and, placing your thumb back in the "V" configuration, tighten up the stitch on the needle.

3 Repeat for the desired number of stitches. The main yarn will form the stitches on the needle and the scrap yarn will make the horizontal ridge at the base of the cast-on row.

4 When picking up the stitches along the cast-on edge, carefully cut and pull out the scrap yarn as you place the exposed loops on the needle.

FRINGE

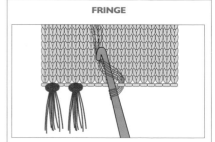

Simple fringe: Cut yarn twice desired length plus extra for knotting. On wrong side, insert hook from front to back through piece and over folded yarn. Pull yarn through. Draw ends through and tighten. Trim yarn.

Knotted fringe: After working a simple fringe (it should be longer to allow for extra knotting), take one-half of the strands from each fringe and knot them with half the strands from the neighboring fringe.

DUPLICATE STITCH

Duplicate stitch covers a knit stitch. Bring the needle up below the stitch to be worked. Insert the needle under both loops one row above and pull it through. Insert it back into the stitch below and through the center of the next stitch in one motion, as shown.

KNIT-ON CAST-ON

1 Make a slip knot on the left needle. *Insert the right needle knitwise into the stitch on the left needle. Wrap the yarn around the right needle as if to knit.

2 Draw the yarn through the first stitch to make a new stitch, but do not drop the stitch from the left needle.

3 Slip the new stitch to the left needle as shown. Repeat from the * until the required number of stitches is cast on.

CHAIN

1 *Pass the yarn over the hook and catch it with the hook.*

2 *Draw the yarn through the loop on the hook.*

3 *Repeat steps 1 and 2 to make a chain.*

SINGLE CROCHET

1 *Insert the hook through top two loops of a stitch. Pass the yarn over the hook and draw up a loop—two loops on hook.*

2 *Pass the yarn over the hook and draw through both loops on hook.*

3 *Continue in the same way, inserting the hook into each stitch.*

HALF-DOUBLE CROCHET

1 *Pass the yarn over the hook. Insert the hook through the top two loops of a stitch.*

2 *Pass the yarn over the hook and draw up a loop—three loops on hook. Pass the yarn over the hook.*

3 *Draw through all three loops on hook.*

DOUBLE CROCHET

1 *Pass the yarn over the hook. Insert the hook through the top two loops of a stitch.*

2 *Pass the yarn over the hook and draw up a loop—three loops on hook.*

SLIP STITCH

Insert the crochet hook into a stitch, catch the yarn, and pull up a loop. Draw the loop through the loop on the hook.

3 *Pass the yarn over the hook and draw it through the first two loops on the hook, pass the yarn over the hook and draw through the remaining two loops. Continue in the same way, inserting the hook into each stitch.*

Illustrations: Joni Coniglio

KNITTING TERMS AND ABBREVIATIONS

approx approximately

beg begin(ning)

bind off Used to finish an edge and keep stitches from unraveling. Lift the first stitch over the second, the second over the third, etc. (UK: cast off)

cast on A foundation row of stitches placed on the needle in order to begin knitting.

CC contrast color

ch chain(s)

cm centimeter(s)

cn cable needle

cont continu(e)(ing)

dc double crochet (UK: tr-treble)

dec decrease(ing)—Reduce the stitches in a row (knit 2 together).

dpn double pointed needle(s)

foll follow(s)(ing)

g gram(s)

garter stitch Knit every row. Circular knitting: Knit one round, then purl one round.

hdc half-double crochet (UK: htr-half treble)

inc increase(ing)—Add stitches in a row (knit into the front and back of a stitch).

k knit

k2tog knit 2 stitches together

lp(s) loops(s)

LH left-hand

m meter(s)

M1 make one stitch—With the needle tip, lift the strand between last stitch worked and next stitch on the left-hand needle and knit into the back of it. One stitch has been added.

MC main color

mm millimeter(s)

oz ounce(s)

p purl

p2tog purl 2 stitches together

pat pattern

pick up and knit (purl) Knit (or purl) into the loops along an edge.

pm place marker—Place or attach a loop of contrast yarn or purchased stitch marker as indicated.

rem remain(s)(ing)

rep repeat

rev St st reverse Stockinette stitch—Purl right-side rows, knit wrong-side rows. Circular knitting: Purl all rounds. (UK: reverse stocking stitch)

rnd(s) round(s)

RH right-hand

RS right side(s)

sc single crochet (UK: dc - double crochet)

sk skip

SKP Slip 1, knit 1, pass slip stitch over knit 1.

SK2P Slip 1, knit 2 together, pass slip stitch over k2tog.

sl slip—An unworked stitch made by passing a stitch from the left-hand to the right-hand needle as if to purl.

sl st slip stitch (UK: single crochet)

ssk slip, slip, knit—Slip next 2 stitches knitwise, one at a time, to right-hand needle. Insert tip of left-hand needle into fronts of these stitches from left to right. Knit them together. One stitch has been decreased.

st(s) stitch(es)

St st Stockinette stitch—Knit right-side rows, purl wrong-side rows. Circular knitting: Knit all rounds. (UK: stocking stitch)

tbl through back of loop

tog together

tr treble crochet (UK: dtr-double treble)

WS wrong side(s)

w&t wrap and turn

wyif with yarn in front

wyib with yarn in back

work even Continue in pattern without increasing or decreasing. (UK: work straight)

yd yard(s)

yo yarn over—Make a new stitch by wrapping the yarn over the right-hand needle. (UK: yfwd, yon, yrn)

* Repeat directions following * as many times as indicated.

[ ] Repeat directions inside brackets as many times as indicated.

Sasha Kagan brings her brand of refreshing naturalism to autumn with this sweet design featuring seed-stitch detailing. Front and back seams create a mirror image, while lace adds subtle elegance to an otherwise whimsical piece.

Instructions are written for one size.

■ Length from neck to point 25½"/65cm
■ Circumference around lower edge 82½"/209.5cm

■ 6 1¾oz/50g balls (each approx 118yd/108m) of Rowan Yarns *Summer Tweed* (silk/cotton) in #515 raffia (MC) (**4**)
■ 1 ball each in #501 lilac (A), #524 cotton bud (B), #509 sunset (C), #530 toast (D), and #508 oats (E)
■ One pair each sizes 3 and 5 (3.25 and 3.75mm) needles *or size to obtain gauge*

20 sts and 23 rows to 4"/10cm over chart pat using larger needles.
Take time to check gauge.

Row 1 (RS) *K1, p1; rep from * to end.

Row 2 *P1, k1; rep from * to end.
Rep these 2 rows for seed st.

(over 10 sts)
Row 1 (RS) K4, yo, k1, ssk, k3.
Row 2 P2, p2tog tbl, p1, yo, p5.
Row 3 K6, yo, k1, ssk, k1.
Row 4 P2tog tbl, p1, yo, p7.
Row 5 K3, k2tog, k1, yo, k4.
Row 6 P5, yo, p1, p2tog, p2.
Row 7 K1, k2tog, k1, yo, k6.
Row 8 P7, yo, p1, p2tog.
Rep rows 1-8 for little vine-lace panel.

1 Poncho is made in two pieces, then seamed up the front and back.
2 It is helpful to use waste yarn to mark the positions of lace patterns.

With smaller needles and MC, cast on 206 sts. Work 6 rows seed st. Change to larger needles.
Beg chart
Working little vine-lace pat as indicated on chart, beg with st 1, work 54 sts of chart 3 times, work first 44 sts once more. AT SAME TIME, shape sides as foll:
Row 1 (RS) K1, k2tog, work to last 3 sts, ssk, k1. **Row 2** P1, p2tog tbl, work to last

3 sts, p2tog, p1. **Row 3** Work even. **Row 4** Rep row 2. **Row 5** Rep row 1. **Row 6** Work even. Rep rows 1-6 until there are 122 sts. Then rep row 1 only every RS row 25 times—72 sts. Work even in chart through row 50.

Eyelet and seed neck edge

With smaller needle and MC, work 2 rows seed st. **Next (eyelet) row** Work 3 sts seed st, yo, k2tog, *work 6 sts seed st, yo, k2tog; rep from * to last 3 sts, work 3 sts seed st. Work 3 more rows in seed st. Bind off in seed st.

Work as for first side, except work chart as mirror image of first side by reading RS rows left to right and WS rows right to left.

Block pieces to measurements. Sew front and back seams. With C, make a 48"/122cm twisted or crochet cord. Thread through eyelet holes at neck.

Color Key

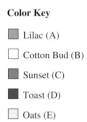

Lilac (A)

Cotton Bud (B)

Sunset (C)

Toast (D)

Oats (E)

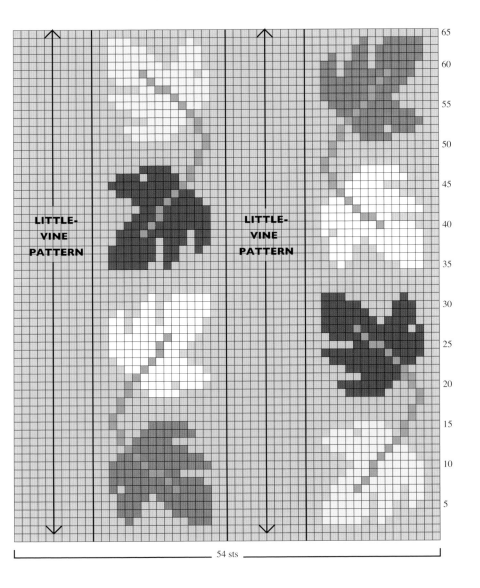

Bias seams and charming crocheted edging make this Veronica Manno design simple and sweet all at the same time.

PONCHO RECTANGLES
(make 2)

Cast on 40 sts and work in St st for 18"/46cm. Bind off.

FINISHING
Block pieces to measurements. Sew cast-on edges of both rectangles to the other rectangle's opposite lower edges to make poncho.

Neck edging

With RS facing and crochet hook, work 2 rnds of sc around neck edge, working 3 sc for every 4 knit rows.

Lower edging

With RS facing and crochet hook, work 1 rnd of sc around lower edge, working 1 sc for every knit st. **Next rnd** *Work 1 sc, skip 1, work 4 sc in next sc; rep from * around.

Liza Prior Lucy gives the basic one-piece poncho a makeover with distinctive stitching and breezy edging. Garter ribbing adds chunky texture while a bobble border brings a touch of flirty fun.

SIZES
Instructions are written for size Small/Medium. Changes for Large/X-Large are in parentheses.

KNITTED MEASUREMENTS
▪ Length from shoulder 20 (24)"/50.5 (61)cm
▪ Width from cast-on to bound-off edge 41½ (52½)"/105.5 (133)cm

MATERIALS
▪ 9 (13) 3½oz/100g (each approx 100yd/90m) of Crystal Palace Yarns *Iceland Solid* (merino wool) in #1219 fuchsia (5)
▪ Size 15 (10mm) circular needle, 29"/74cm long *or size to obtain gauge*
▪ 2 long stitch holders
▪ Size P/15 (10mm) crochet hook

GAUGE
12 sts and 17 rows to 4"/10cm over garter rib using size 15 (10mm) needle.
Take time to check gauge.

NOTE
Poncho is knit sideways.

STITCH GLOSSARY
MB (Make Bobble) K into the front, back, front, back, front of st, turn; k5, turn; p5, turn; k2tog, k1, k2tog, turn; k3tog.

BOBBLED GARTER RIB
(multiple of 2 sts plus 6)
Row 1 (RS) Knit.
Row 2 *K1, p1; rep from * to end.
Row 3 K2, MB, k to last 3 sts, MB, k2.
Row 4 *K1, p1; rep from * to end.
Rep rows 1-4 for bobbled garter rib.

PONCHO
Cast on 120 (144) sts. Work in bobbled garter rib for 17 (22)"/43 (56)cm, end with a WS row.
Split for neck
Next row Work 60 (72) sts, slip these sts on holder, work to end—60 (72) sts. Work even in pat as established for 31 (35) rows, place these sts on holder. **Next row** Slip sts from first holder back to needle and attach yarn at neck edge. Work even in pat as established for 31 (35) rows.
Close neck
Next row (RS) K across all 120 (144) sts. Work even in pat as established for 17 (22)"/43 (56)cm, end with RS row. Bind off knitwise.

Block to measurements, allowing outside
edges to curl to inside. With RS facing and
crochet hook, work 1 rnd backwards SC
(from left to right) evenly.

This light and airy Irina Poludnenko design is softly sensual in mohair. Bobbles add femininity, as does the garment's asymmetrical drape.

SIZES
Instructions are written for one size.

KNITTED MEASUREMENTS
- Length 55"/139.5cm
- Width 19"/48cm

MATERIALS
- 4 .88oz/25g balls (each approx 151yd/138m) of GGH Muench Yarns *Kid Soft* (super kid mohair/nylon/wool) in #55 light pink (4)
- One pair size 8 (5mm) needles *or size to obtain gauge*

GAUGE
16 sts and 20 rows to 4"/10cm over St st using size 8 (5mm) needles.
Take time to check gauge.

STITCH GLOSSARY
5-in-1 Bobble K1, yo, k1, yo, k1 in one st, turn. K5, turn. K5, turn. K2tog, k1, k2tog, turn. P3tog—1 st rem. Place this st on RH needle.

PONCHO RECTANGLE
Cast on 76 sts and work in St st for 18"/46cm. Work in St st, making randomly spaced groups of 6 or 7 bobbles—see photo. Work even until piece measures 55"/139.5cm from beg. Bind off all sts very loosely.

FINISHING
Fold the rectangle and sew the cast-on edge to the side edge, making a poncho.

■■■▭

This ethnic-inspired style is anything but square! Designed by Christine L. Walter, it combines bold geometry and delicate openwork for a wonderful warm-weather wearable.

Instructions are written for one size.

KNITTED MEASUREMENTS

■ Each panel approx 17" x 29"/43cm x 74cm

MATERIALS

■ 8 1¾oz/50g balls (each approx 85yd/78m) of Berroco, Inc. *Cotton Twist Colors* (cotton/rayon) in #8464 morandi mix (MC) (**4**)

■ 5 1¾oz/50g balls (each approx 85yd/78m) of Berroco, Inc. *Cotton Twist* (cotton/rayon) in #8373 clay (CC) (**4**)

■ Size 8 (5mm) circular needle, 29"/74cm long *or size to obtain gauge*

■ Stitch holder

■ Size E/4 (3.5mm) crochet hook

GAUGE

18 sts and 36 rows to 4"/10 cm over garter stitch using size 8 (5mm) needle.
Take time to check gauge.

STRIPED GARTER PATTERN

Rows 1 and 2 With MC, k1 tbl, k to last st, sl st purlwise wyif.

Rows 3 and 4 With CC, k1 tbl, k to last st, sl st purlwise wyif.

Rep rows 1-4 for striped garter pat.

STRIPED GARTER AND LACE PATTERN

Row 1 (RS) With MC, k1 tbl, k to last st, sl st purlwise wyif.

Row 2 K1 tbl, k to last st, sl st purlwise wyif.

Rows 3, 4, 5, and 6 Rep rows 1 and 2 twice.

Row 7 With CC, rep row 1.

Row 8 K1 tbl, p1, *yo, p2tog; rep from * to last st, sl st purlwise wyif.

Rep rows 1-8 for striped garter and lace pat.

NOTE

Always k first st tbl and sl last st purlwise wyif.

PANEL

(make two)

With MC, cast on 157 sts. **Preparation row** K1 tbl, k to end. Work striped mitered square as foll: **Dec row 1 (RS)** K1 tbl, k76, k3tog, k76, sl last st purlwise wyif.

Row 2 K1 tbl, k to last st, sl last st purlwise wyif. Beg striped garter pat, AT SAME TIME, cont to work dec row every RS row, working one less before and after center double decrease. Cont in this way until 1 st rem, end with RS row. **Next row** With RS of work facing and last stitch (in MC) still on needle, pick up and knit 78 sts along left side of mitered square—79 sts. **Next row** Beg striped garter and lace pat, starting with row 2, then work even for total of 12 reps of 8-row pat. With MC, K 6 rows. Break yarn, leaving approx 36"/91.5cm for grafting. Sl to holder.

Make second panel and leave sts on needle.

Graft end of second panel to right side edge of mitered square on first panel. Sl sts of first panel from holder and graft to right side edge of mitered square on second panel.

Edging

Using MC and crochet hook, work a single row of backwards sc (from left to right) around edges at both neck and lower edge of poncho.

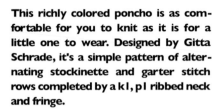

This richly colored poncho is as comfortable for you to knit as it is for a little one to wear. Designed by Gitta Schrade, it's a simple pattern of alternating stockinette and garter stitch rows completed by a k1, p1 ribbed neck and fringe.

SIZES

Instructions are written for size 2-3. Changes for 3-4, 5-6, and 7-8 are in parentheses.

KNITTED MEASUREMENTS

■ Length from shoulder 11½ (13¾, 15¾, 18)"/29 (35, 40, 46)cm

■ Length from center back neck 14¼ (17, 19½, 22)"/36 (43, 49.5, 56)cm

■ Circumference around lower edge 46½ (54, 61, 68)"/118 (137, 155, 172.5)cm

MATERIALS

■ 1 (2, 2, 2) 1¾oz/50g ball(s) (each approx 135yd/123m) of Naturally/S.R. Kertzer *Allsorts* (wool/polyester) in #402 cobalt (A) and #400 red (B) ③

■ 1 (1, 1, 2) ball(s) each in #405 purple (C) and #403 navy (D)

■ 1 (1, 2, 2) ball(s) in #401 jade (E)

■ One pair each size 3 and 5 (3.25mm and 3.75mm) needles *or size to obtain gauge*

■ Stitch holders

■ Size F/5 (3.75mm) crochet hook

GAUGE

22 sts and 30 rows to 4"/10cm over St st using size 5 (3.75mm) needles.
Take time to check gauge.

PATTERN STITCH

Work 4 rows garter st, 8 rows St st, 4 rows garter st. Rep these 16 rows for pat st.

STRIPE PATTERN

Work 16 rows each A, B, C, D, E; rep these 80 rows for stripe pat.

PONCHO

(make two panels)

With smaller needles and E, cast on 128 (148, 168, 188) sts. Work 4 rows garter st. Cont in pat st and stripe pat as foll:

Beg pats and shaping

Next (dec) row (RS) K1, SKP, work to last 3 sts, k2tog, k1. Work 3 rows even. Change to larger needles. Rep dec row on next row, then every other row 41 (50, 58, 67) times more—42 (44, 48, 50) sts. Place sts on holder for turtleneck.

FINISHING

Block pieces to measurements. Sew center front seam.

Turtleneck

Place sts from both holders onto one smaller needle—84 (88, 96, 100) sts. With RS facing and last color used, work in k1, p1 rib for ¾"/2cm. Change to larger needles and next color. Cont to work in rib, change colors every 9th row until neckband measures 4¾ (4¾, 5½, 5½)"/12 (12, 14, 14)cm, end with a WS row. Bind off very loosely (use larger needles if necessary). Sew center back and turtleneck seam.

Fringe

Cut 5½ (6, 6¼, 6¾)"/14 (15, 16, 17)cm lengths of yarn in each color. Use crochet hook to attach single-color 3-strand fringes on every other k1 rib along bound-off edge of neckband, placing colors randomly.

Bring in the funk with this cool cropped poncho designed by Gayle Bunn. The chic look is quick to achieve using circular needles and working in a k5, p5 rib.

SIZES

Instructions are written for size Small/Medium. Changes for Large/X-Large are in parentheses.

KNITTED MEASUREMENTS

■ Length (without fringe) 16½ (18½)"/42 (47)cm

■ Circumference around lower edge 55 (61½)"/139 (156)cm

MATERIALS

■ 4 (5) 3½ oz/100g hanks (each approx 173yd/158m) of Colinette Yarns/Unique Kolours *Tagliatelli* (merino wool/nylon) in #135 sahara (⑤)

■ Size 11 (8mm) circular needle, 29"/74cm long *or size to obtain gauge*

■ Set of four or five size 11 (8mm) double pointed needles

■ Size K/10.5 (6.5mm) crochet hook for attaching fringe

GAUGE

13 sts and 16 rows to 4"/10cm over k5, p5 rib using size 11 (8mm) needles.
Take time to check gauge.

PONCHO

With circular needle, cast on 180 (200) sts loosely. Join, being careful not to twist sts and pm to indicate beg of rnd.

Beg rib pat

Next rnd *P5, k5; rep from * around. Rep last rnd for rib pat until work measures 8 (9)"/20.5 (23)cm from beg.

Shape yoke

Note Change to set of four (or five) needles when necessary to accommodate sts.

Rnd 1 *P5, k2, k2tog, k1; rep from * around—162 (180) sts.

Rnds 2-8 *P5, k4; rep from * around.

Rnd 9 *P2, P2tog, p1, k4; rep from * around—144 (160) sts.

Rnds 10-16 *P4, k4; rep from * around.

Rnd 17 *P4, k1, k2tog, k1; rep from * around—126 (140) sts.

Rnds 18-20 *P4, k3; rep from * around.

Rnd 21 *P1, p2tog, p1, k3; rep from * around—108 (120) sts.

Rnds 22-24 *P3, k3; rep from * around.

Rnd 25 *P3, k1, k2tog; rep from * around—90 (100) sts.

Rnds 26 and 27 *P3, k2; rep from * around.

Rnd 28 *P1, p2tog, k2; rep from * around—72 (80) sts.

Rnd 29 *P2, k2; rep from * around.

Rnd 30 *P2tog, k2, p2, k2; rep from * around—63 (70) sts.

Rnds 31-34 *P1, k2, p2, k2; rep from * around. Bind off size Small/Medium only, loosely in pat.

Size L/XL only

Rnd 35 *P1, k2, p2tog, k2, p1, k2, p2, k2; rep from * around—65 sts

Rnds 36-38 *P1, k2, p1, k2, p1, k2, p2, k2; rep from * around.

Bind off loosely in pat.

Fringe

Cut 11"/28cm lengths of yarn. Use crochet hook to attach 4-strand fringes in every 5th st around lower edge as shown. Trim fringe evenly.

Irina Poludnenko proves that zippers aren't just for jackets anymore! Fun and functional, this cabled beauty also features shaping that gives any pair of shoulders lovely definition.

SIZES

Instructions are written for size Small. Changes for Medium and Large are in parentheses.

KNITTED MEASUREMENTS

▨ Length 18 (20, 21)"/46 (51, 53)cm

▨ Circumference at lower edge 45½ (48½, 51½)"/115.5 (123, 131)cm

▨ Circumference at neck 19 (20, 21)"/48 (51, 53)cm

MATERIALS

▨ 8 (9, 10) 1¾oz/50g balls (each approx 77yd/70m) of Filatura di Crosa *Zara Plus* (merino wool) #7 light blue ▨**5**▨

▨ Size 9 (5.5mm) circular needle, 29"/74cm long *or size to obtain gauge*

▨ Cable needle (cn)

▨ Stitch holders

▨ Size I/9 (5.5mm) crochet hook

▨ One separating zipper 18 (20, 21)"/46 (51, 53)cm long

GAUGES

▨ 14 sts and 20 rows to 4"/10cm over St st using size 9 (5.5mm) needle.

▨ 17 sts and 20 rows to 4"/10cm over cable pat using size 9 (5.5mm) needle.
Take time to check gauges.

STITCH GLOSSARY

6-st BC Sl 3 sts to cn and hold to *back*, k3, k3 from cn.

6-st FC Sl 3 sts to cn and hold to *front*, k3, k3 from cn.

CABLE PATTERN

[multiple of 14 (15, 16) sts plus 9]

Row 1 (RS) K9, *p5 (6, 7), k9; rep from * to end.

Row 2 and all WS rows P9, *k5 (6, 7), p9; rep from * to end.

Row 3 6-st FC, k3, *p5 (6, 7), 6-st FC, k3; rep from * to end.

Row 5 Rep row 1.

Row 7 K3, 6-st BC, *p5 (6, 7), k3, 6-st BC; rep from * to end.

Row 8 Rep row 2.

Rep rows 1-8 for cable pat.

PONCHO

Cast on 193 (206, 219) sts. Working first and last st in St st for selvage, work in cable pat for 12 (13, 14)"/30.5 (33, 35.5)cm, ending with a WS row.

Divide for fronts, back, and shoulder

Next row (RS) Work 43 (46, 49) sts and place on holder for right front; work 9 sts in cable pat, increasing 1 st in first and last st (for selvage) and place on holder for side edge; work 89 (96, 103) sts in cable pat and place on holder for back; work 9 sts in cable pat, increasing 1 st in first and last sts (for selvage) and place on holder for side edge; work 43 (46, 49) sts in cable pat for left front.

LEFT FRONT
Next row (WS) Work even.
Shoulder shaping
Bind off 4 (3, 4) sts at beg of next row. Cont to bind off 4 (3, 4) sts at same edge 6 (9, 7) times more—15 (16, 17) sts rem. Work 1 row even. Place on holder.

BACK
Next row (WS) Work 89 (96, 103) sts from holder in cable pat as established.
Shoulder shaping
Bind off 4 (3, 4) sts at beg of next 14 (20, 16) rows—33 (36, 39) sts rem. Place on holder.

RIGHT FRONT
Next 2 rows Slip 43 (46, 49) sts from holder to needle and work 2 rows in cable pat as established.
Shoulder shaping
Bind off 4 (3, 4) sts at beg of next WS row, then cont to bind off 4 (3, 4) sts at same edge 6 (9, 7) times more—15 (16, 17) sts rem. Place on holder.

SHOULDER STRIPS
(make two)
Work 11 sts from holder in cable pat for 32 rows and place on holder.

TURTLENECK
Sew shoulder strips to fronts and back.
Next row (RS) Work across 15 (16, 17) sts from right front holder, 11 sts from shoulder strip holder, decreasing 1 st in first and last st, 33 (36, 39) sts from back holder, 11 sts from shoulder strip holder, decreasing 1 st in first and last st; and 15 (16, 17) sts from left front holder—81 (86, 91) sts. Work in cable pat as established for 3"/7.5cm. Bind off all sts in pat.

FINISHING
Block to measurements.
Front edges
Work 1 row sc, then 1 row backwards sc (from left to right).
Sew in zipper.

Put some shimmer in your step with this creation from Irina Poludnenko. It's the staple stockinette glammed up with a little shine and a touch of fuzzy faux fur.

SIZES

Instructions are written for size Small. Changes for Medium and Large are in parentheses.

KNITTED MEASUREMENTS

- Length from shoulder 20"/51cm
- Circumference at lower edge 50 (53, 56)"/127 (134.5, 142)cm

MATERIALS

- 4 (5, 5) 1¾oz/50g balls (each approx 90yd/81m) of Trendsetter *Dune* (mohair/acrylic/viscose/nylon/metal) in #80 orange green (A) 🔲
- 1 1¾oz/50g balls (each approx 180yds/165m) in Trendsetter *Voilà* (nylon) in #17 wine (B) 🔲
- Size 10 (6mm) circular needles, 16" and 29"/40 and 74cm long *or size to obtain gauge*
- Set of 4 or 5 size 10 (6mm) double pointed needles (dpns)
- Stitch marker
- Stitch holders

GAUGE

12 sts and 16 rows to 4"/10cm over St st and A using size 10 (6mm) needle.
Take time to check gauge.

NOTE

Poncho is worked in the round from the bottom up.

PONCHO

With two strands B held tog, cast on 150 (160, 170) sts. Pm for beg of rnd and join, being sure not to twist sts. Work 4 rnds garter st (k 1 rnd, p 1 rnd). Change to A and k 12 rnds.

Armholes

Next row K40 sts, turn. **Next row** P40, turn. Working on only these 40 sts, work 20 rows of St st. Cut yarn and leave 40 sts on holder. Rejoin yarn and work 20 rows of St st on rem 110 (120, 130) sts. **Next 12 rnds** Join 40 sts from holder and 110 (120, 130) sts and work even in St st. **Next rnd** *K15 (16, 17), pm; rep from * around.

Next (dec) rnd **K2tog, k to next marker; rep from ** around—140 (150, 160) sts. Work 2 rnds even. Rep last 3 rnds 9 times more, changing to shorter needles when necessary—50 (60, 70) sts.

Collar

Work k1, p1 rib for 10 rnds. Cut yarn.
With 2 strands B held together, work 4
rnds garter st. Bind off loosely.

With dpns and 2 strands B held tog, pick
up and knit 38 sts around armholes. Work
4 rnds garter st. Bind off.

Heather Lodinsky's Alice in Wonderland design is a great introduction to a technique that you'll be able to use for years to come. In this case it employs multiple sizes of squares for a psychedelic look.

SIZES

Instructions are written for size Small/ Medium. Changes for size Large/X-Large are in parentheses.

KNITTED MEASUREMENTS

■ Length 19 (21½)"/48 (54.5)cm without fringe

■ Circumference at lower edge 60 (69)"/152 (175)cm

MATERIALS

■ 4 (5) 1¾oz/50g skeins (each approx 100yd/91m) of Knit One, Crochet Too *Meringue* (merino wool/viscose/polymide) in #845 Cafe au Lait (A) and #841 fawn (B) (4)

■ Size 8 (5mm) circular needle, 32"/ 80cm long *or size to obtain gauge*

■ Size I/9 (5.5mm) crochet hook

GAUGE

16 sts and 24 rows to 4"/10cm over St st using size 8 (5mm) needle.
Take time to check gauge.

PONCHO

Make bottom rectangles With A, *cast on 14 (15) sts. Work in garter st for 28 (30) rows. Break yarn (leaving approx 6"/15.5cm end), slide sts to end of needle. Rep from * 11 (13) times more—12 (14) garter st rectangles on needle.

Make second (X-leaning) set of rectangles With last worked rectangle near tip of right needle, use B to pick up 13 (14) sts along left edge of rectangle. Without turning, slide rectangle closest to left needle to tip of left needle, and k1 st. With tip of left needle, bring last picked-up st over top of st just knit [there should be 13 (14) sts in B on needle]. **Turn entire work, p13 (14), turn. K12 (13), sl 1, k1 from left rectangle, psso. Rep from ** until last row includes last st from left rectangle, ending with RS facing. Without turning or breaking B, pick up 13 (14) sts down left side of rectangle now on right needle and attach to next rectangle and work same as previous rectangle. Cont to work rectangles until there are 12 (14) rectangles and work is joined together (last row should include live sts of first rectangle that was picked up).

Make third (X-leaning) set of rectangles Break B, leaving end and turn work. With A and right needle, pick up purlwise 12 (13) sts along left edge of rectangle on right needle. P1 from next rectangle on left needle, and pass last st picked up over this st [there should be 12 (13) sts in A on right needle]. ***Turn, k12 (13). Turn, purl p 11 (12), sl1, p1 from next rectangle and psso. Rep from *** until last purl row works last st of left rectangle. Without turning, pick up 12 (13)-sts purlwise down left side of rectangle just joined. Work 11 (13) more rectangles in A, until twelve (fourteen) 12 (13) st rectangles have been worked. Break A, turn. With B, pick up 11 (12) sts down left side of rectangle on right needle and join to next as first round of B rectangles. Cont to work rectangles back and forth in the round, picking up one fewer st in each succeeding round until last round is worked with A (B) and 4 sts. When last 4-st rectangle is worked, turn to RS, ****bind off 4 sts on left needle, then pick up 4 sts down left side of each rectangle, binding off after each picked-up st. Rep from **** until all sts and picked-up sts have been bound off. Tie off last st.

FINISHING

For each of the 12 (14) tassels, cut four 12"/30.5cm strands of each color and fold in half. With crochet hook, attach each tassel to bottom of each rectangle as pictured.

Perfect for a day of leaf-peeping and apple-picking, this Alison Green Will design intertwines classic cabling and durable fiber for a look that is both rugged and rustic.

STITCH GLOSSARY

6-st BC Sl 3 sts to cn and hold to *back*, k3, k3 from cn.

6-st FC Sl 3 sts to cn and hold to *front*, k3, k3 from cn.

M1R Insert LH needle from back to front under horizontal strand between the two needles. K into front of the strand.

M1L Insert LH needle from front to back under horizontal strand between the two needles. K into back of the strand.

CABLE PATTERN

(multiple of 14 sts)

Rnds 1 and 2 *P2, k12; rep from * around.

Rnd 3 *P2, 6-st FC, 6-st BC; rep from * around.

Rnds 4, 5, and 6 *P2, k12; rep from * around.

Rep rnds 1-6 for cable pat.

NOTE

Poncho is worked in the round from the neck down.

PONCHO

With shorter needle, cast on 80 sts. Pm and join, being careful not to twist sts. Work 4 rnds garter st (k one rnd, p one rnd). **Next rnd** *P2, k1, (M1, k2) 3 times, M1, k1; rep from * 7 times more—112 sts.

Change to larger needle. Work in cable pat, working 6 rnds of pat 5 times (30 rnds).

Beg shaping

Note Use 2nd color markers to indicate inc points. Change to longer needle when necessary.

Inc rnd 1 *P2, k12, p2, pm, M1R, k12, M1L, pm; rep from * 3 times more—120 sts. **Rnd 2** Work 1 rnd even. **Inc rnd 3 (cable)** *P2, 6-st FC, 6-st BC, p2, M1R, k14, M1L; rep from * 3 times more—128 sts. **Rnd 4** Work 1 rnd even. **Inc rnd 5** *Work to first marker, sl marker, M1R, work to next marker, M1L, sl marker; rep from * 3 times more—136 sts. **Rnd 6** Work 1 rnd even. Cont in pats, rep last 2 rnds 22 times more, then work inc rnd 5 every 4th rnd 13 times more; AT SAME TIME, work cables as established every 6th rnd—416 sts. Bind off in pat.

FINISHING

Cut 8"/20.5cm lengths of yarn for fringe. Use crochet hook to attach 4-strand fringes approx 1"/2.5 cm apart along lower edge of poncho.

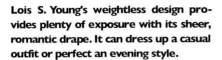

Lois S. Young's weightless design provides plenty of exposure with its sheer, romantic drape. It can dress up a casual outfit or perfect an evening style.

SIZES

Instructions are written for one size.

KNITTED MEASUREMENTS

■ Length from back of neck 36"/91.5cm (without fringe)
■ Width 56"/142cm (without fringe)

MATERIALS

■ 10 .88oz/25g (each approx 110yd/100m) of Le Fibre Nobili/Plymouth Yarns *Imperiale* (mohair/nylon) in #4123 light green (5)
■ Size 10 (6 mm) circular needle, 29"/74cm long *or size to obtain gauge*
■ Size F/5 (3.75mm) crochet hook
■ Stitch markers

GAUGE

12 sts and 16 rows to 4"/10 cm over lace pat using size 10 (6mm) needle.
Take time to check gauge.

NOTES

1 The first st of each row is slipped as if to p, making a chained edge.
2 When working into double yo, work first st as k and second st as p.

3 Mohair is best worked on bamboo needles.

STITCH GLOSSARY

M1R Insert LH needle from back to front under horizontal strand between the two needles. K into front of the strand.

M1L Insert LH needle from front to back under horizontal strand between the two needles. K into back of the strand.

FRONT LACE PATTERN

(multiple of 4 sts plus side edge increases)
Row 1 (RS) Sl 1, M1R, k3, *k2tog, yo twice, ssk; rep from * to last 4 sts, end k3, M1L, k1.
Row 2 Sl 1, k4, *p1, (k1, p1) in double yo, p1; rep from * to last 5 sts, end k5.
Row 3 Sl 1, M1R, k to last st, end M1L, k1.
Row 4 Sl 1, k4, p to last 5 sts, end k5.
Work rows 1-4 for front lace pat.

BACK LACE PATTERN

(multiple of 4 sts plus side edge decreases)
Row 1 (RS) Sl 1, ssk, k3, *k2tog, yo twice, ssk; rep from * to last 5 sts, end k2, k2tog, k1.
Row 2 Sl 1, k4, *p1, (k1, p1) in double yo, p1; rep from * to last 5 sts, end k5.
Row 3 Sl 1, ssk, k to last 3 sts, end k2tog, k1.
Row 4 Sl 1, k4, p to last 5 sts, end k5.
Work rows 1-4 for back lace pat.

FRONT

Cast on 2 sts very loosely. K 1 row. Sl 1, M1R, M1L, k1. **WS rows** Sl 1, k to end of row. **RS rows** Sl 1, M1R, k to last st, M1L, k1. Work these two rows until there are 12 sts, end with WS row. Work front lace pat until there are 88 sts, end with RS row.

Next row Work 40 sts in pat, pm, k8, pm, work 40 sts.

Next row Cont in pat for 8 rows, working center 8 sts in garter st.

Note On row 1, if last st before marker is k2tog, work it as k2tog, yo; work center k8; then yo, k2tog, and finish row.

Divide for front opening

Work to first marker, k4, attach a second ball of yarn, k4 to marker, work to end. Work back and forth on the two halves of front in pat as established, working chained edge on center opening (see first note). Cont until there are 65 sts in each half of front, end with a RS row.

Next row Work to 20 sts before neck edge, pm, k20, removing first marker. On second half, k20, removing marker and placing it after the 20 k sts. Work 8 rows in pat as established, with the 20 sts next to neck edges worked in garter st.

Neck

Next 2 rows Bind off 16 sts at each neck edge (one side on RS, the other on WS), working pat as established—53 sts each side.

Next 4 rows Work pat as established, but do NOT work M1R or M1L at poncho edges. Work 1 more row, ending with a WS.

Join back neck

Work across back, casting on 32 sts between the halves as foll: Cast on each st by working a M1R and giving it an extra twist before putting it on left-hand needle. Join to second half of back and finish row—138 sts. Work 8 rows in back lace pat, working garter sts between markers. Remove markers and work entire row in back lace pat. Cont until 12 sts rem. End lace pat. Work all sts in garter st and cont to dec at edges. When 2 sts rem, k2tog, bind off.

Neck edging

Using crochet hook, work sl st edging as foll: Work sl st in first st, *ch 1, work sl st in next 2 sts; rep from *.

Attach yarn to each neck corner and work 6"/15cm-long chains for ties.

Fringe

Cut 17"/43cm lengths of yarn. Starting at side corner, use crochet hook to attach 4-strand fringe to edge, then make a second knot in fringe 1"/2.5cm from edge knot. Cont to attach fringes on every other edge stitch. Trim fringe evenly.

■■■■▶

Gayle Bunn gets cable-ready with this thick and intricate design featuring a broad collar and ribbed edging. Working on chunky circular needles, you'll knit it up in no time!

SIZES

Instructions are written for one size.

KNITTED MEASUREMENTS

- Length to collar 18"/45.5cm
- Lower edge circumference 70"/178cm

MATERIALS

- 6 3½oz/100g balls (each approx 117yd/107m) of Filtes King/Needful Yarns *Van Dyck* (wool/acrylic/alpaca) in # 334 blue 🅢
- Size 10½ (6.5mm) circular needle, 16"/40cm long
- Size 15 (8mm) circular needles, 16 and 24"/40 and 60cm long *or size to obtain gauge*
- Cable needle (cn)

GAUGE

12 sts and 19 rows to 4"/10cm over St st using larger needles.
Take time to check gauge.

STITCH GLOSSARY

4-st BPC Sl 1 st to cn and hold to *back*, k3, p1 from cn.

4-st FPC Sl 3 sts to cn and hold to *front*, p1, k3 from cn.

5-st BPC Sl 1 st to cn and hold to *back*, k4, p1 from cn.

5-st BPC kdec Sl 1 st to cn and hold to *back*, k1, k2tog, k1, then p1 from cn.

5-st FPC Sl 4 sts to cn and hold to *front*, p1, k4 from cn.

5-st FPC kdec Sl 4 sts to cn and hold to *front*, p1, then (k1, k2tog, k1) from cn.

4-st FPC dec Sl 2 sts to cn and hold to *back*, k3, then p2tog from cn.

4-st BC Sl 2 sts to cn and hold to *back*, k2, k2 from cn.

4-st FC Sl 2 sts to cn and hold to *front*, k2, k2 from cn.

6-st BC Sl 3 sts to cn and hold to *back*, k3, k3 from cn.

6-st FC Sl 3 sts to cn and hold to *front*, k3, k3 from cn.

8-st BC Sl 4 sts to cn and hold to *back*, k4, k4 from cn.

8-st FC Sl 4 sts to cn and hold to *front*, k4, k4 from cn.

CABLE-RIB PATTERN

(multiple of 29 sts)

Rnds 1 and 2 *P3, k4, p4, k8, p4, k4, p2; rep from * around.

Rnd 3 *P3, k4, p4, 8-st BC, p4, k4, p2; rep from * around.

Rnds 4-8 Rep rnd 1.

Rep rnds 1-8 for cable-rib pat.

PONCHO

With larger circular needle, cast on 164 sts. Pm to indicate beg of rnd and join, making sure not to twist sts. Work 6 rnds in k2, p2 rib. **Next (inc) rnd** Cont in rib as established, inc 39 sts evenly around— 203 sts. Work 3½ reps of cable-rib pat, end with row 4.

Note Change to shorter circular needle when necessary during shaping.

Work rnds 1 to 38 of woven cable chart— 70 sts.

Change to smaller needle. **Rnd 1** *K2, p2; rep from * to last 6 sts, end k1, k2tog, p1, p2tog—68 sts. **Rnds 2-6** *K2, p2; rep from * around.

Split for collar

Row 1 [K2, p2] 8 times, k1 (center front). Turn. Work back and forth across needle in rows. **Row 2 (WS)** P1, *k2, p2; rep from * to last 3 sts, k2, p1. **Row 3** K1, *p2, k2; rep from * to last 3 sts, p2, k1.

Rep rows 2 and 3 until collar measures 6½"/16.5cm from beg. Bind off in rib.

Stitch Key

☐	K on RS rows, P on WS rows
⊟	P on RS rows, K on WS rows
	8-st FC
	6-st FC
	5st BPC
	5-st FPC
	K2 tog
	P2tog
	5-st FPC Kdec
	5-st BPC Kdec
	4-st FC
	4-st BC
	4-st BPC
	4-st FPC
	5-st BPC pdec
	5-st FPC kdec
☐	No stitch

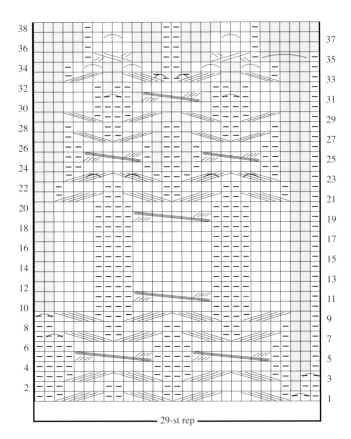

Shiny ribbon-tape yarn transforms Diane Zangl's design from traditional to sensational! It's merely worked in basic stockinette stitch with eyelet detailing.

SIZES

Instructions are written for size Small/Medium. Changes for Large are in parentheses.

KNITTED MEASUREMENTS

■ Length 15 (16)"/38 (40.5)cm without fringe
■ Neck circumference 20 (21)"/51 (53)cm
■ Lower edge circumference 63 (74½)"/160 (189)cm

MATERIALS

■ 7 (9) 1¾oz/50g balls (each approx 110yd/100m) of Lion Brand *Incredible* (nylon) in #206 autumn leaves ⑤
■ Size 9 (5.5mm) circular needles, 16"/40cm and 29"/73.5cm long *or size to obtain gauge*
■ Stitch markers
■ Size H/8 (5mm) crochet hook

GAUGE

15 sts and 18 rows to 4"/10cm over St st using size 9 (5.5mm) needles.
Take time to check gauge.

NOTE

Capelet is worked from the neck down.

CAPELET

Cast on 76 (80) sts. Pm and join, being careful not to twist sts. P 1 rnd, placing 3 more markers after every 19th (20th) st. K 1 rnd, p 1 rnd.

Next (inc) rnd *K to 1 st before marker, yo, k1, sl marker, k1, yo; rep from * around—84 (88) sts.

Next rnd Rep last 2 rnds 19 (24) times, changing to longer needles when necessary—236 (280) sts. Work even until piece measures 14 (15)"/35.5 (38)cm from beg. Work in garter st (k 1 rnd, p 1 rnd) for 1"/2.5cm.

Loop bind-off

Bind off 2 sts, *make a 1½"/4cm loop over finger, bind off 2 sts, remove loop from finger; rep from * around.

FINISHING

Neck edging

With RS facing and crochet hook, work 1 rnd backwards sc (from left to right) evenly around neck edge. Join with sl st and fasten off.

Alison Green Will stays down to earth with a mossy-green style worked in the round for easy completion. The clover-leaf stitch makes for a lush pattern that can be worn diagonally or vertically.

SIZES

Instructions are written for one size.

KNITTED MEASUREMENTS

■ Length from center neck to tip 26"/66cm

■ Width at widest point 32"/81cm

MATERIALS

■ 8 1¾oz/50g balls (each approx 109yd /100m) of Cherry Tree Hill *Possum Paints Worsted* (merino/possum) in loden

■ Size 7 (4.5mm) circular needle, 29"/74cm long *or size to obtain gauge* (4)

■ Size F/5 (3.75mm) crochet hook

GAUGE

19 sts and 26 rows to 4"/10cm over cloverleaf pattern using size 7 (4.5mm) needle.
Take time to check gauge.

CLOVERLEAF PATTERN

(multiple of 6 sts plus 7)

Row 1 and all WS rows K2, *p3, k1, P1 tbl, k1; rep from * to last 5 sts, p3, k2.

Row 2 (RS) P2, *yo, SK2P, yo, p1, k1 tbl, p1; rep from * to last 5 sts, yo, SK2P, yo, p2.

Row 4 P2, *k1, yo, ssk, p1, k1 tbl, p1; rep from * to last 5 sts, k1, yo, ssk, p2.

Row 6 P2, *k3, p1, k1 tbl, p1; rep from * to last 5 sts, k3, p2.

Rep rows 1-6 for cloverleaf pat.

PICOT CROCHET EDGING

*Work 3 sc, ch 3, sl st into base of chain; rep from * around.

PONCHO PANEL

(Make one)

Cast on 79 sts. Do not join. Rep rows 1-6 of cloverleaf pat 31 times, work row 1 once more—piece measures approx 29"/73.5cm from beg.

Using cable cast-on method, cast on 55 sts at beg of next row—134 sts. Cont cloverleaf pat as foll:

Row 2 P1, k1 tbl, p1, *yo, sk2p, yo, p1, k1 tbl, p1; rep from * to last 5 sts, yo, sk2p, yo, p2.

Rows 3, 5, and 7 K1, pl tbl, k1, *p3, k1, pl tbl, k1; rep from * to last 5 sts, p3, k2.

Row 4 P1, k1 tbl, p1, *k1, yo, ssk, p1, k1 tbl, p1; rep from * to last 5 sts, k1, yo, ssk, p2.

Row 6 P1, k1 tbl, p1, *k3, p1, k1 tbl, p1; rep from * to last 5 sts, k3, p2. Rep 2-7 rows 17 times more. Bind off in pat.

Block piece to measurements. Mark positions A, B, C, E, F at corners as per diagram. Mark point D 16"/40cm from cast-on edge. Pin point C to point D and point B to point F, and sew seam from C/D to B/F.

Edging

Work picot crochet border around neck and lower edges, working 1 sc into each st on cast-on and bind-off edges, and working 3 sc for every 4 rows on side edges. Fasten off.

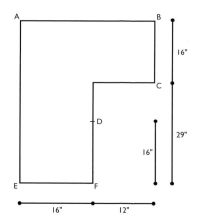

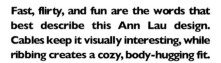

Fast, flirty, and fun are the words that best describe this Ann Lau design. Cables keep it visually interesting, while ribbing creates a cozy, body-hugging fit.

SIZES

Instructions are written for one size.

KNITTED MEASUREMENTS

- Length 24"/61cm
- Circumference at lower edge 68"/ 172.5cm

MATERIALS

- 6 3½oz/100g skeins (each approx 78yd/71m) of Patons *Up Country* (wool) in #80913 deep oak (6)
- Size 15 (10mm) circular needle, 16"/40cm and 24"/60cm long *or size to obtain gauge*
- Cable needle (cn)
- Stitch markers (2 colors—1 for beg of rnd, 1 for inc)

GAUGE

10 sts and 14 rows to 4"/10cm over St st using size 15 (10mm) needle.
Take time to check gauge.

STITCH GLOSSARY

8-st FC Sl 4 sts to cn and hold to *front*, k4, k4 from cn.

2-RND BIND-OFF

Rnd 1 K1, p1, pass k st over p st. Cont in this way to the end of rnd, keeping all sts on RH needle.
Rnd 2 Slip 2 sts purlwise, pass first slipped st over 2nd. Cont until 1 st rem and bind off.

NOTE

Poncho is worked in the round from the neck down.

PONCHO

With shorter needle, cast on 52 sts. Pm to mark beg of rnd and join, being sure not to twist sts. Work 12 rnds in k2, p2 rib.

Shaping

Note Use 2nd color markers to indicate inc points. Change to longer needle when necessary.
Next (setup) rnd K8, pm, p2, k2, p2, pm, k6, M1, pm, p2, k2, M1, k2, M1, k2, p2, pm, M1, k6, pm, p2, k2, p2, pm, k8, M1, k2, pm, M1—58 sts. **Next rnd** K to marker, sl marker, p2, k2, p2, sl marker, k to next marker, sl marker, p2, k8, p2, sl marker, k to next marker, sl marker, p2,

k2, p2, sl marker, k to end of rnd. **Next (inc) rnd** K to marker, sl marker, p2, k2, p2, sl marker, k to next marker, M1, sl marker, p2, k8, p2, sl marker, M1, k to next marker, sl marker, p2, k2, p2, sl marker, k to next marker, M1, k2, M1—62 sts. Rep last 2 rnds once, then work 1 rnd even, 66 sts. **Next (cable) rnd** K to marker, sl marker, p2, k2, p2, sl marker, k to next marker, M1, sl marker, p2, 8-st FC, p2, sl marker, M1, k to next marker, sl marker, p2, k2, p2, sl marker, k to next marker, M1, k6, M1—70 sts. Cont to work in pat as established, working cable rnd every 10th rnd and inc rnd every other rnd to 178 sts. Bind off using 2-rnd bind-off method.

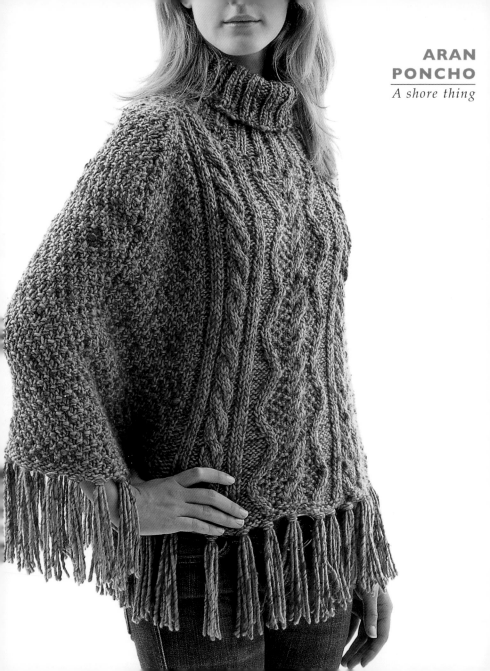

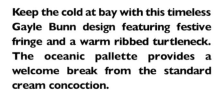

Keep the cold at bay with this timeless Gayle Bunn design featuring festive fringe and a warm ribbed turtleneck. The oceanic pallette provides a welcome break from the standard cream concoction.

SIZES

Instructions are written for size Small/Medium. Changes for Large/X-Large are in parentheses.

KNITTED MEASUREMENTS

■ Length to shoulder (not including fringe) 18½ (20¼)"/47 (51.5)cm
■ Circumference at lower edge 56 (60)"/142 (152)cm

MATERIALS

■ 8 (9) 1¾oz/50g skeins (each approx 94yd/86m) of Classic Elite *Gatsby* (wool/viscose/nylon) in #2146 blue/green (**5**)
■ Size 10½ (6.5mm) circular needle, 29"/74cm long *or size to obtain gauge*
■ Size 9 (5.5mm) circular knitting needle 16"/40cm long
■ Cable needle (cn)
■ Stitch holders
■ Size K/10½ (6.5mm) crochet hook (for attaching fringe)

GAUGE

12 sts and 19 rows to 4"/10cm over Irish moss st with larger needles.
Take time to check gauge.

STITCH GLOSSARY

3-st BC Sl 1 st to cn and hold to *back*, k2, k1 from cn.

3-st FC Sl 2 sts to cn and hold to *front*, k1, k2 from cn.

3-st BPC Sl 1 st to cn and hold to *back*, k2, p1 from cn.

3-st FPC Sl 2 sts to cn and hold to *front*, p1, k2 from cn.

6-st BC Sl 3 sts to cn and hold to *back*, k3, k3 from cn.

6-st FC Sl 3 sts to cn and hold to *front*, k3, k3 from cn.

IRISH MOSS ST

(over an odd number of sts)
Row 1 (RS) K1, *p1, k1; rep from * to end.
Row 2 P1, *k1, p1; rep from * to end.
Row 3 P1, *k1, p1; rep from * to end.
Row 4 K1, *p1, k1; rep from * to end.
Rep rows 1-4 for Irish moss st.

RIGHT CABLE

(over 6 sts)

Row 1 (RS) 6-st BC.

Rows 2 and 4 P6.

Rows 3 and 5 K6.

Row 6 P6.

Rep rows 1-6 for right cable pat.

LEFT CABLE

(over 6 sts)

Row 1 (RS) 6-st FC.

Rows 2 and 4 P6.

Rows 3 and 5 K6.

Row 6 P6.

Rep rows 1-6 for cable pat.

CABLE PANEL

(over 20 sts)

Row 1 (RS) P3, 3-st BC, p1, 6-st BC, p1, 3-st FC, p3.

Row 2 K3, p2, k1, p8, k1, p2, k3.

Row 3 P2, 3-st BPC, k1, p1, k6, p1, k1, 3-st FPC, p2.

Row 4 K2, p3, k1, p8, k1, p3, k2.

Row 5 P1, 3-st BC, p1, k1, p1, k6, p1, k1, p1, 3-st FC, p1.

Row 6 K1, p2, [k1, p1] twice, p6, [p1, k1] twice, p2, k1.

Row 7 3-st BPC, [k1, p1] twice, 6-st BC, [p1, k1] twice, 3-st FPC.

Row 8 P3, [k1, p1] twice, p6, [p1, k1] twice, p3.

Row 9 3-st FPC, [k1, p1] twice, k6, [p1, k1] twice, 3-st BPC.

Row 10 K1, p2, [k1, p1] twice, p6, [p1, k1] twice, p2, k1.

Row 11 P1, 3-st FPC, p1, k1, p1, k6, p1, k1, p1, 3-st BPC, p1.

Row 12 K2, p3, k1, p8, k1, p3, k2.

Row 13 P2, 3-st FPC, k1, p1, 6-st BC, p1, k1, 3-st BPC, p2.

Row 14 K3, p2, k1, p8, k1, p2, k3.

Row 15 P3, 3-st FPC, p1, k6, p1, 3-st BPC, p3.

Row 16 K4, p12, k4.

Rep Rows 1-16 for cable panel, turning center 6-st cable every 6 rows as established.

NOTE

Poncho is worked back and forth on a circular needle in two pieces, then sewn together. The collar is worked in the round.

BACK

With larger needle, cast on 85 (91) sts. Do NOT join. Knit 3 rows (note: first row is WS). Change to Irish moss st and work even until piece measures 7½ (8½)"/19 (21.5)cm, end with a WS row.

Shape sides

Next (dec) row K1, ssk, work to last 3 sts, k2tog, k1. Rep dec row every 4th row 9 (10) times more—65 (69) sts. Work 1 row even.

Shoulder shaping

Bind off 3 sts at beg of next 8 (6) rows, 4 sts at beg of next 4 (6) rows. Place rem 25 (27) sts on holder.

FRONT

With larger needles, cast on 85 (91) sts. Knit 3 rows (note: first row is WS) and inc 17 sts evenly across last row—102 (108) sts.

Set-up patterns

Row 1 (RS) P0 (1), [k1, p1] 11 (12) times, k1, p2, k2, p2, work row 1 of left cable, p2, k2, p2, work row 1 of cable panel; p2, k2, p2, work row 1 of right cable, p2, k2, p2, [k1, p1] 11 (12) times, k1, p0 (1). **Row 2** K0 (1), [p1, k1] 11 times, p1, k2, p2, k2, work row 2 of left cable, k2, p2, k2, work row 2 of cable panel, k2, p2, k2, work row 2 of right cable, k2, p2, k2, [p1, k1] 11 (12) times, p1, k0 (1).

Row 3 K0 (1), [p1, k1] 11 (12) times, p3, k2, p2, work row 3 of left cable, p2, k2, p2, work row 3 of cable panel across next 20 sts, p2, k2, p2, work row 3 of right cable, p2, k2, p2, [p1, k1] 11 (12) times, p1, k0 (1). **Row 4** P1 (0), [k1, p1] 11 (12) times, k3, p2, k2, work row 4 of left cable, k2, p2, k2, work row 4 of cable panel, k2, p2, k2, work row 4 of right cable, k2, p2, k2, [k1, p1] 11 (12) times, k1, p0 (1). These 4 rows form Irish moss st pat on sides. Cables are now in position. Cont in pats as established until piece measures 7½"/19cm from beg, ending with WS row.

Shape sides

Next (dec) row K1, ssk, work to last 3 sts, k2tog, k1. Rep dec row every 4th row 9

times more—82 (88) sts. Work 1 row even.

Front neck and shoulder shaping

Bind off 3 sts. Pat across 26 (28) sts (including st on needle after bind-off) (neck edge). Turn. Leave rem sts on a spare needle. Dec 1 st at neck edge on next 9 (10) rows; AT SAME TIME, bind off 3 sts at shoulder edge every other row 3 (2) times, then 4 sts 2 (3) times. With RS facing, slip next 24 (26) sts onto a st holder, join yarn to rem 29 (31) sts and pat to end of row. Bind off 3 sts at shoulder edge on next and foll alt rows 3 (2) times more, then 4 sts 2 (3) times; AT SAME TIME, dec 1 st at neck edge on next 9 (10) rows.

Sew side and shoulder seams.

Collar

With RS facing and smaller circular needle, pick up and k12 sts down left front neck edge, k24 (26) sts from front st holder, decreasing 5 sts evenly across, pick up and k12 sts up right front neck edge, k25 (27) from back st holder—68 (72) sts. Join and work in k2, p2 rib for 8½"/21.5cm. Bind off loosely in rib.

Fringe

Cut 10"/25.5cm lengths of yarn. Use crochet hook to attach 4-strand fringes approx 1"/2.5 cm apart along lower edge of poncho. Trim fringe evenly.

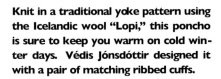

Knit in a traditional yoke pattern using the Icelandic wool "Lopi," this poncho is sure to keep you warm on cold winter days. Védis Jónsdóttir designed it with a pair of matching ribbed cuffs.

SIZES

Instructions are written for one size.

KNITTED MEASUREMENTS

■ Length from shoulder 23"/58cm
■ Circumference at bottom approx 84"/214cm

MATERIALS

■ 6 3½oz/100g balls (each approx 109yd/100m) of Reynolds/Álafoss *Lopi* (icelandic wool) in #9975 black tweed (A) ⑤
■ 2 balls in #0054 ash heather (B)
■ Size 7 (4.5mm) circular needle 16"/40cm long
■ Size 10/6mm circular needles 16 and 29"/40 & 74cm long *or size to obtain gauge*
■ Set of 5 size 7 (4.5mm) double pointed needles (dpns)

GAUGE

13 sts and 18 rnds to 4"/10cm over St st with larger needles.
Take time to check gauge.

NOTE

This poncho is worked in St st in the round (k every rnd) from the neck down.

SEED STITCH

Rnd 1 *K1, p1; rep from * around.
Rnd 2 *P1, k1; rep from * around.
Rep rnds 1 and 2 for seed stitch.

PONCHO

With A and smaller circular needle, cast on 70 sts. Pm and join, making sure not to twist sts. Work k1, p1 rib for 3"/7cm. Change to larger needle size and knit 1 rnd; AT SAME TIME, inc 5 sts evenly around—75 sts.

Work color chart in St st with A and B, and changing to longer needle when necessary, increase as directed on rnds 3, 6, 10, 18, and 23—200 sts.

At end of chart, break off B and work with A only. Work 2 rnds even.
Next rnd *K8, M1; rep from * around—225 sts. Work 20 rnds even.
Next rnd *K9, M1; rep from * around—250 sts. Work 20 rnds even.
Next rnd *K10, M1; rep from * around—275 sts. Work 5 rnds even or until desired length.
Next 5 rnds Work seed st. Bind off loosely. Weave in all ends.

(make two)

With A and dpns, cast on 28 sts. Join and work in k1, p1 rib for 4"/10cm. Bind off loosely. Weave in ends.

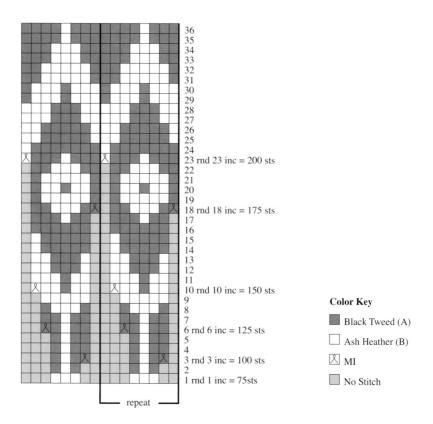

36
35
34
33
32
31
30
29
28
27
26
25
24
23 rnd 23 inc = 200 sts
22
21
20
19
18 rnd 18 inc = 175 sts
17
16
15
14
13
12
11
10 rnd 10 inc = 150 sts
9
8
7
6 rnd 6 inc = 125 sts
5
4
3 rnd 3 inc = 100 sts
2
1 rnd 1 inc = 75sts

repeat

Color Key

■ Black Tweed (A)

☐ Ash Heather (B)

⋉ MI

▨ No Stitch

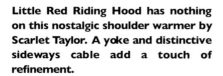

Little Red Riding Hood has nothing on this nostalgic shoulder warmer by Scarlet Taylor. A yoke and distinctive sideways cable add a touch of refinement.

SIZES

Instructions are written for size Small/Medium. Changes for Large/X-Large are in parentheses.

KNITTED MEASUREMENTS

■ Length (not including fringe) 16"/40.5cm

■ Width at lower edge 49½ (55)"/125.5 (139.5)cm

MATERIALS

■ 4 (5) 3½oz/100g skeins (each approx 223yd/204m) of Patons Yarn *Classic Merino Wool* (wool) in #208 burgundy (4)

■ Size 7 (4.5mm) circular needle, 29"/74cm long *or size to obtain gauge*

■ One pair size 5 (3.75mm) needles

■ Cable needle

■ Stitch markers

■ One ¾"/20mm button (shown with JHB International #1823)

GAUGE

20 sts and 26 rows to 4"/10cm over St st using larger needles.

Take time to check gauge.

STITCH GLOSSARY

6-st BC Sl 3 sts to cn and hold to *back*, k3, k3 from cn.

6-st FC Sl 3 sts to cn and hold to *front*, k3, k3 from cn.

SIDEWAYS-CABLE BORDER PATTERN

(over 20 sts)

Rows 1 and 3 (RS) P2, k9, p2, k7.

Row 2 and all WS rows P7, k2, p9, k2.

Row 5 P2, 6-st FC, k3, p2, k7.

Rows 7 and 9 Rep row 1.

Row 11 P2, k3, 6-st BC, p2, k7.

Row 12 Rep row 2.

Rep rows 1-12 for cable border pat.

FAUX POCKET-TRIM CABLE PATTERN

(over 13 sts)

Row 1 (RS) P2, k9, p2.

Row 2 and all WS rows K2, p9, k2.

Row 3 P2, 6-st FC, k3, p2.

Row 5 Rep row 1.

Row 7 P2, k3, 6-st BC, p2.

Row 8 Rep row 2.

Rep rows 1-8 for cable pocket trim.

Capelet is worked back and forth in one piece on circular needle.

SIDEWAYS-CABLE BORDER

With circular needle, cast on 20 sts. Work cable border pat until piece measures 49½ (55)"/125.5 (139.5)cm from beg, end with row 4.

Create fringe

Next row (RS) Bind off first 13 sts, unravel rem 7 sts across and all the way down to cast-on edge. Cut the loops. Use overhand knots to tie two strands tog for each fringe. Trim fringe edges evenly.

CAPE

With circular needle and RS facing, pick up and knit 248 (288) sts evenly along side edge of cabled piece opposite fringe. K1 row. Beg with a RS row, work even in St st for 5 rows. **Next (setup) row** P62 (72), pm, p124 (144), pm, p62 (72). **Next (dec) row (RS)** Work to 2 sts before first marker, SKP, sl marker, k2tog, work to 2 sts before next marker, SKP, sl marker, k2tog, work to end—244 (284) sts. Rep dec row every 8th row 7 (8) times more—216 (252) sts. Work even until piece measures 12 (14)"/30.5 (35.5)cm from beg, end with a WS row.

Shoulder and yoke shaping

Next (dec) row K1, [k2tog, k1] 17 (20) times, SKP, sl marker, k2tog, k2, k2tog, [k1, k2tog] 33 (39) times, k1, SKP, sl marker, k2tog, [k1, k2tog] 17 (20) times, k1—144 (168) sts. Work even for 11 (13) rows. **Next (dec) row** [K1, k2tog] 11 (13) times, k1, SKP, sl marker, k2tog, k2, k2tog, [k1, k2tog] 21 (25) times, k1, SKP, sl marker, k2tog, k1, [k2tog, k1] 11 (13) times—96 (112) sts. Work even until piece measures 15¾ (18)"/40 (45.5)cm from beg, end with a WS row. **Next (dec) row** [K3, k2tog] 4 (5) times, k2 (1), SKP, sl marker, k2tog, k1, [k3, k2tog] 8 (10) times, k3 (1), SKP, sl marker, k2tog, k2 (1), [k2tog, k3] 4 (5) times—76 (88) sts. Work 1 row even.

Neckband

Next row Change to smaller needles and work in k2, p2 rib for approx 1"/2.5cm. Bind off loosely in rib.

FINISHING

Button band

With RS facing, and smaller needles, pick up and k 90 (98) sts evenly along left front edge. Work in k2, p2 rib until band measures 1"/2.5cm. Bind off loosely in rib.

Pm for one button ½"/1.5mm from top edge.

Buttonhole band

With RS facing, and smaller needles, pick up and k 90 (98) sts evenly along right front edge. Work in k2, p2 rib until band measures approx ½"/1.5cm. **Next (buttonhole) row** Make one buttonhole working (yo, k2tog) opposite marker. Cont in k2, p2 rib as established until band measures 1"/2.5cm. Bind off loosely in rib.

Faux pocket trims

(make two)

With larger needles, cast on 13 sts and work faux pocket-trim cable pat until piece measures approx 3½"/9cm, end with row 8 of pat. Bind off loosely.

Pin trims approx 2"/5cm from front edge and 1¾"/4.5cm from lower edge of cape on left and right fronts, sew in place.

Sew button opposite buttonhole.

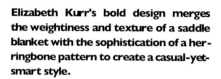

Elizabeth Kurr's bold design merges the weightiness and texture of a saddle blanket with the sophistication of a herringbone pattern to create a casual-yet-smart style.

SIZES

Instructions are written for one size.

KNITTED MEASUREMENTS

▨ Length from center neck to tip (not including fringe) approx 26"/66cm

▨ Circumfence at widest 58"/147cm

MATERIALS

▨ 5 skeins 8oz/226g (each approx 132yd/121m) of Brown Sheep Co.'s *Burly Spun* (wool) in #BS180 ruby red ⑥

▨ 1 skein 4oz/113g (each approx 125yd/114m) of Lamb's Pride *Bulky* wool/mohair #M180 red ⑤

▨ One pair size 15 (10mm) needles *or size needed to obtain gauge*

▨ Size 15 (10mm) circular needle, 24"/60cm long

▨ Size N/10mm crochet hook

GAUGE

11 stitches and 17 rows to 4½"/11.5cm in herringbone pat.
Take time to check gauge.

STITCH GLOSSARY

K1Btbl From the top, insert point of right-hand needle into the purl bump of the st below next st on lefthand needle and knit it, k the next st—1 st inc.

HERRINGBONE PATTERN

(Multiple of 7 sts, plus 2)

Rows 1 and 3 (WS) Sl 1 purlwise, p to end.

Row 2 Sl 1 knitwise, *k2tog, k2, K1Btbl, k2; rep from* to last 4 sts, k4.

Row 4 Sl 1 knitwise, k3, *K1Btbl, k2, k2tog, k2; rep from* to last 3 sts, k2tog, k1.
Repeat Rows 1-4 for herringbone pat.

PROVISIONAL CAST-ON

1 Using cotton waste yarn of a similar weight, crochet a chain the same number of stitches required for cast-on, plus 2, fasten off loosely.

2 Working through back ridge of chain, pick up and k desired number of stitches.

3 When ready to work sts, pull tail to "unzip" chain and put live sts back on needle.

SINGLE CROCHET BIND-OFF

Using crochet hook, sl first st off needle, *insert crochet hook into next st on left-hand needle as if to knit, yo, pull loop through st on needle and on hook, letting st drop off needle; rep from*. Fasten off.

(make two)

Cast on 38 sts using provisional cast-on.
Work herringbone pat until piece measures
30"/76cm from beg. Bind off, using single
crochet method.

Remove waste yarn from provisional cast-
on, slipping sts to needle. Join yarn and
bind off, using single crochet method

FINISHING

Block pieces. Sew 15"/38cm of cast-on
edge of one rectangle along 15"/38cm at
side edge of 2nd rectangle.

Neck

With RS facing and circular needle, pick
up and k46 sts evenly around neckline.
Join and k4 rnds. Bind off using regular
method.

Bottom Edge

With RS facing, sc evenly around, working 2 sc in the st before and after each corner. Fasten off.

Fringe

Cut 14"/35.5cm lengths of yarn. Use crochet hook to attach 2-strand fringes in
every other sc around lower edge. Trim
fringe evenly.

Get openminded with **Alison Green Will's** cable-and-mesh coverup, a sizzling look for spring and summer worked in bamboo, the latest in fiber technology.

SIZES

Instructions are written for size Small/Medium. Changes for Large/X-Large are in parentheses.

KNITTED MEASUREMENTS

▨ Length of rectangle 29 (32)"/74 (81)cm

▨ Width of rectangle 17 (19)"/43 (48)cm

▨ Length from center neck to tip 24 (26¾)"/61 (68)cm

MATERIALS

▨ 4 (5) 3½oz/100g balls (each approx 250yd/229m) of South West Trading Company *Bamboo* (bamboo) in #521 sapphire 🔳

▨ One pair size 5 (3.5mm) needles *or size to obtain gauge*

▨ Size E/4 (3.5mm) crochet hook

▨ Cable needle

GAUGE

27 sts and 30 rows to 3.5"/9cm over cable chart using size 5 (3.5mm) needles.

Take time to check gauge.

STITCH GLOSSARY

3-st BPC Sl 1 st to cn and hold to *back*, k2, p1 from cn.

3-st FPC Sl 2 sts to cn and hold to *front*, p1, k2 from cn.

4-st FC Sl 2 sts to cn and hold to *front*, k2, k2 from cn.

4-st BC Sl 2 sts to cn and hold to *back*, k2, k2 from cn.

RECTANGLE

(make two)

Cast on 93 (103) sts.

Beg chart

Row 1 (WS) P12 (16), work row 1 of cable chart over next 27 sts, p15 (17), work row 1 of cable chart over next 27 sts, p12 (16). **Row 2** K2, [yo, k2tog] 5 (7) times, work row 2 of cable chart over next 27 sts, k1, [yo, k2tog] 7 (8) times, work row 2 of cable chart over next 27 sts, k1 [yo, k2tog] 5 (7) times, k1. **Row 3** P12 (16), work row 3 of cable chart over next 27 sts, p15 (17), work row 3 of cable chart over next 27 sts, p12 (16). **Row 4** K1 [ssk, yo] 5 (7) times, k1, work row 4 of cable chart over next 27 sts, [ssk, yo] 7 (8) times, k1, work row 4 of cable chart over next 27 sts, [ssk, yo] 5 (7) times, k2. Cont in pat as established, work 16 rows of cable chart 15 (16) times, then rep rows 1-8 of chart once more. Bind off in pat.

FINISHING

Block pieces to measurements. Sew 17 (19)"/43 (48)cm of cast-on edge of one rectangle along 17 (19)"/43 (48)cm at side edge of 2nd rectangle.

Edgings

Work sc around neck and lower edge, working 1 sc into each st on cast-on and bind-off edges, and working 2 sc for every 3 rows on side edges.

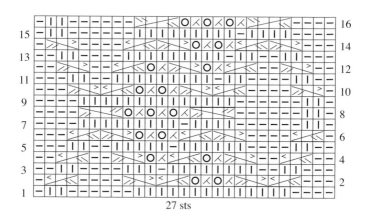

27 sts

Stitch Key

	K on RS, p on WS
	P on RS, k on WS
	Slip 1 st to CN and hold to back, k2, p1 from CN
	Slip 2 sts to CN and hold to front, p1, k2 from CN
	K2tog
	Yarn over
	Slip 2 sts to CN and hold to front, k2, k2 from CN
	Slip 2 sts to CN and hold to back, k2, k2 from CN

RESOURCES

US RESOURCES

Write to the yarn companies listed below for purchasing and mail-order information.

BERROCO, INC.
14 Elmdale Road
P.O. Box 367
Uxbridge, MA 01569

BROWN SHEEP CO.
100662 County Road 16
Mitchell, NE 69357

CASCADE YARNS
1224 Andover Park E
Tukwila, WA 98188-3905

CHERRY TREE HILL YARNS
PO Box 659
Barton VT 05822

CLASSIC ELITE YARNS
122 Western Ave.
Lowell, MA 01851

COLINETTE YARNS
distributed by
Unique Kolours

CRYSTAL PALACE
160 23rd Street
Richmond, CA 94804

FILATURA DI CROSA
distributed by
Tahki•Stacy Charles, Inc.

GGH
distributed by
Muench Yarns

ISTEX
distributed by
S.R. Kertzer, LTD

KARABELLA YARNS
1201 Broadway
New York, NY 10001

KNIT ONE CROCHTE TWO
91 Tandberg Trail, Unit 6
Windham, ME 04062

LA FIBRE NOBILI
distributed by
Plymouth Yarns

LION BRAND YARN CO.
34 West 15th Street
New York, NY 10011

MUENCH YARNS
1323 Scott Street
Petaluma, CA 94954

NATURALLY
distributed by
S. R. Kertzer, Ltd.

NEEDFUL YARNS
4476 Chesswood Drive
Suite 10 & 11
Tornoto, ON M3J 2B9

PATON® YARNS
PO Box 40
Listowel, ON N4W3H3

PLYMOUTH YARN
PO Box 28
Bristol, PA 19007

ROWAN YARNS
4 Townsend West, Unit 8
Nashua, NH 03063

SOUTHWEST TRADING CO,.
1867 E. Third Street ste 2
Tempe, AZ 85281

S. R. KERTZER, LTD
50 Trowers Road
Woodbridge ON L4L7K6
Canada

TAHKI•STACY CHARLES, INC.
70-30 80th Street
Building #36
Ridgewood, NY 11385

TRENDSETTER YARNS
16742 Stagg Street
Suite 104
Van Nuys, CA 91406

UNIQUE KOLOURS
28 N. Bacton Hill Road
Malvern, PA 19355

CANADIAN RESOURCES

Write to US resources for mail-order availability of yarns not listed.

BERROCO, INC.
distributed by
S. R. Kertzer, Ltd.

CLECKHEATON
distributed by
Diamond Yarn

DIAMOND YARN
9697 St. Laurent
Montreal, PQ H3L 2N1
and
155 Martin Ross, Unit #3
Toronto, ON M3J 2L9

LES FILS MUENCH, CANADA
5640 rue Valcourt
Brossard, Quebec
J4W 1C5 Canada

MUENCH YARNS, INC.
distributed by
Les Fils Muench, Canada

NATURALLY
distributed by
S. R. Kertzer, Ltd.

PATONS ®
PO Box 40
Listowel, ON N4W 3H3

ROWAN
distributed by
Diamond Yarn

S. R. KERTZER, LTD.
105A Winges Rd.
Woodbridge, ON L4L 6C2

UK RESOURCES

Not all yarns used in this book are available in the UK. For yarns not available, make a comparable substitute or contact the US manufacturer for purchasing and mail-order information.

ROWAN YARNS
Green Lane Mill
Holmfirth
West Yorks HD7 1RW
Tel: 01484-681881

SILKSTONE
12 Market Place
Cockermouth
Cumbria, CA13 9NQ
Tel: 01900-821052

THOMAS RAMSDEN GROUP
Netherfield Road
Guiseley
West Yorks LS20 9PD
Tel: 01943-872264

VOGUE KNITTING PONCHOS

Editorial Director
TRISHA MALCOLM

Graphic Designer
MATT DOJNY

Art Director
CHI LING MOY

Stylist
RACHAEL STEIN

Executive Editor
CARLA S. SCOTT

Book Manager
ERICA SMITH

Instructions Editor
KAREN GREENWALD

Production Manager
DAVID JOINNIDES

Yarn Editor
VERONICA MANNO

Photography
JACK DEUTSCH STUDIOS

Assistant Editor
MIRIAM GOLD

President, Sixth&Spring Books
ART JOINNIDES